# My Marriage, My D.E.S.T.I.N.Y.

## 7 Keys to Leave a Legacy of Love

Tonya Loving Collins

My Marriage, My D.E.S.T.I.N.Y © Copyright <<2021>> Tonya Loving Collins All rights reserved. No part of this publication may be reproduced, distributed, or transmitted in any form or by any means, including photocopying, recording, or other electronic or mechanical methods, without the prior written permission of the publisher, except in the case of brief quotations embodied in critical reviews and certain other noncommercial uses permitted by copyright law.

Scriptures taken from www.biblegateway.com, versions as indicated in the text. All rights reserved worldwide.

Although the author and publisher have made every effort to ensure that the information in this book was correct at press time, the author and publisher do not assume and hereby disclaim any liability to any party for any loss, damage, or disruption caused by errors or omissions, whether such errors or omissions result from negligence, accident, or any other cause.

Adherence to all applicable laws and regulations, including international, federal, state, and local governing professional licensing, business practices, advertising, and all other aspects of doing business in the US, Canada, or any other jurisdiction is the sole responsibility of the reader and consumer.

Neither the author nor the publisher assumes any responsibility or liability whatsoever on behalf of the consumer or reader of this material. Any perceived slight of any individual or organization is purely unintentional.

The resources in this book are provided for informational purposes only and should not be used to replace the specialized training and professional judgment of a health care or mental health care professional.

Neither the author nor the publisher can be held responsible for the use of the information provided within this book. Please always consult a trained professional before making any decision regarding treatment for yourself or others.

For more Information, email info@crowningdesinies.com.

# TAKE YOUR "FREE" LOVE QUIZ!

To get the best experience with this book, I've found readers who complete this free Love Quiz are able to implement the strategies faster and take the next steps needed toward a fulfilling relationship.

If you haven't already taken it, you can access it by visiting the free resources page at:

**www.crowningdestinies.com**

## Dedication

This book is dedicated to the loves of my life:

Russ, I am so grateful for God allowing our paths to intersect. One thing's for sure. There has never been a dull moment since the day we met. Every birthday and other special moments have been nothing short of spectacular since the day you entered my life. Of course, every day of the decades we've shared together was not all sunny—that would be inhumane. I can, however, honestly say the good times by far outweigh any challenge we've had to contend with. You are a beautiful person inside and out, and I am so grateful for the opportunity to "do life" with you. We have traveled the world together—sharing so many experiences throughout the United States and abroad. I am especially grateful for the two lives God blessed us with, a perfect blend of us.

Rashelle and Rashon, no one could have ever prepared me for the unconditional love I would experience as your mother. We have a unique bond and a special love that only a mother and a daughter can share. You have loved me from the start and never allowed circumstances to interrupt your unwavering love and support of me. It is my prayer that this book will not only make a difference in your lives, but also impact the lives of your children and your children's children for many years to come. I always wanted to give you my very best, and I salute you with this book as a testament to what is possible when you believe and are willing to do the work. Thank you for being my heartbeats and the fuel behind my "why."

LaTavia and Tavarus, you have added color to my life and challenged me in ways I never thought possible over the many years I've watched you grow from childhood to adulthood. You introduced me to motherhood and inspire me to constantly self-reflect and level up to be a better version of myself. I love you both more than you'll ever know.

And to those of you who still have an ounce of hope to believe in love and desire to get the most out of your marriages, may this book reignite you to have a lifetime of greater fulfillment in your relationships.

# Table of Contents

Preface .................................................................. 13

Chapter 1: INTRODUCTION .............................. 15

Chapter 2: DREAMING ....................................... 21

Chapter 3: EMPATHY ......................................... 33

Chapter 4: SELF-AWARENESS .......................... 45

Chapter 5: THANKFULNESS ............................. 57

Chapter 6: INTEGRITY ....................................... 67

Chapter 7: NEWNESS ......................................... 79

Chapter 8: YEARNING ....................................... 89

Chapter 9: REFLECTIONS: The God Factor ...... 99

Acknowledgements ............................................. 108

About the Author ................................................ 110

Endnotes ............................................................. 117

# Preface

After spending decades in marriage enrichment and witnessing decades of heartbreak, I began observing potential gaps in the marriage material I reviewed. I looked closely at how useful and applicable it was to—not only my marriage, but also other marriages. More often than not, I always felt incomplete like "something" was missing that I was seeking.

My life philosophy has always been to avoid criticizing anything I am unable or unwilling to offer a feasible solution to. And that's when *My Marriage, My D.E.S.T.I.N.Y.* was birthed. It offers a fresh perspective on making marriage thrive for a lifetime and allows me to influence and bless individuals and couples beyond my immediate reach.

I took my experience and established the disciplines necessary to impact my life and marriage—as well as the countless marriages of others on the journey. I know it will radically shift your relational perspective and transform your relationship. Regardless of where you are in your marriage, application of the practical strategies in this book will enable you to be the author of your life and create the marriage you've always dreamed of. Your destiny and family legacy awaits!

My Marriage, My D.E.S.T.I.N.Y.

# Chapter 1: INTRODUCTION

*Our greatest joy and our greatest pain come in our relationships with others.*

STEPHEN R. COVEY[i]
Educator, Businessman, Keynote Speaker, and Author of *The 7 Habits of Highly Effective People*

Is it even possible to stay "in love" forever? We all know falling in love is easy despite how complicated the world is today. You know...those days when you didn't want to spend a second apart, and when you were apart, you were on the phone or communicating by some other means. You literally came alive when in each other's presence. Everything seemed nearly perfect, and you didn't have a care in the world. So, why does staying in love seem to be a far-fetched fantasy? Staying in love challenges even the best of relationships over time, and many find themselves anticipating when the spark will go out. I even remember thinking to myself early on, *Russ will*

# INTRODUCTION

*be this charming for how long?* After all, he was in fact the perfect gentleman who catered to me right from the start.

The same things that intrigue us in the beginning stages seem to loathe us later in our relationships. Unfortunately, marriages also fall into this category. They do not stay the same. Actually, nothing stays the same. Things will either get better or things will get worse over time. You eventually enter a crossroad and must decide whether to advance or retreat after moving past the "in-love" experience which research shows lasts approximately two years at best. I also remember wondering earlier in my marriage how couples could stay married for decades and still end up in divorce court, but I later learned that children often complicate the equation. Consequently, many couples "tolerate" each other for longer so as not to inconvenience or inflict any unnecessary hardship on their children.

We place a deeper expectation on our intimate relationships than on any other relationship. In fact, our intimate relationships play a vital role in

My Marriage, My D.E.S.T.I.N.Y.

our overall happiness even if we have fulfillment in every other area of our lives. Whether married or single many of us fear that we won't be loved "intimately" despite receiving love from other sources such as our parents, children, or friends.

Sadly, a 2018 study revealed that 86 percent of married couples are not happy. And according to author Dana Adam Shapiro, only about 17 percent of married people are happy.[ii] Still another poll found that about six in ten couples are unhappily married, four out of ten say they have considered leaving their partner, and one in ten no longer trusts their partner.

Why is it that those butterflies we feel early on that lead us to the altar seem to fade away over time? Marriage obviously requires work, but you have to be working on the right things. *My Marriage, My D.E.S.T.I.N.Y* provides seven practical strategies you can easily implement in your relationship (and life) to attract a more satisfying and fulfilling relationship.

After years and years of bringing counsel to

## INTRODUCTION

others struggling in their relationships, watching my extended family devastated by divorce, and personally being married, divorced, and remarried again for decades now, I have seen firsthand what works and what doesn't work. It truly breaks my heart to see so many couples living a superficial life of frustration and daily disappointment mainly due to a lack of relationship fulfillment. Still others make the difficult decision to part ways far too soon after the "in love" stage disappears. Shockingly, couples typically do not divorce because they stop loving each other—they divorce because they no longer have the passion and intimacy they once knew.

Yet there is little, if any, regard to how the children may be affected—if there are any children. Children often experience mental health, academic, and even behavioral challenges when confronted with divorce at a young age. There may also be additional strain regarding acceptance of future relationships if the children do not receive positive intervention. Nonetheless, we ignore the significance and long-term impact our relationship decisions

## My Marriage, My D.E.S.T.I.N.Y.

have on our families and on our legacy. This is most likely due to a failure to look beyond current frustration and discomfort and develop the appropriate tools to choose a better-informed alternative.

Do you realize that one day you will be an ancestor? It's time to start thinking about something more than just your immediate gratification and understand how your relationship today will affect generations to come. How would you feel if you knew you were sowing seeds to positively impact the relationships of future generations? Yes, one day you will actually be an ancestor. My question to you is: What legacy are you leaving behind? A legacy of spontaneous decision-making or a legacy of impact-driven decision-making? Given the residual effects of divorce, it is time we take a more proactive approach to our relationships. Each and every one of us has a defined expiration, so why not live a life that purposely provides an example to others?

It has been proven time and again that we are more likely to do things for others than we are

# INTRODUCTION

for ourselves. That probability is even greater when it involves our children. From waking up for late-night feedings and diaper changes to supporting every game, we do it even when we do not feel like it. And don't think your children stop watching your example when they become adults.

This book will delve into how applying the seven key strategies of D.E.S.T.I.N.Y. will help you create a legacy of love by focusing on shared Dreams, demonstrating Empathy, being Self-Aware, expressing Thankfulness, having unshakeable Integrity, keeping things New and igniting a Yearning for your mate. Since "the quality of your life is the quality of your relationships," (Tony Robbins), make it an immediate priority to learn the tools necessary to leave a marital legacy. Generations are depending on you to be the agent of change.

My Marriage, My D.E.S.T.I.N.Y.

## Chapter 2: DREAMING

*The future belongs to those who believe in the beauty of their dreams.*

ELEANOR ROOSEVELT
Former First Lady of the United States

What's the point of dreaming when dreams rarely come true anyway? Far too many people stop dreaming at some point in their lives because they feel they're too old or too young, or it becomes too risky to chase their dreams. It is even more common to find couples who do not share dreams. Nonetheless, dreaming is the first strategy and a crucial one because it gives relationships purpose and direction. In order to get to where you're going, you have to know your current position. Think about it—if someone is giving you directions, they normally use your starting position as a point of reference. Hence, it is beneficial to begin your marriage with a non-negotiable, desired endstate in mind. When Russ and I were engaged to marry, I told him jokingly – but

## DREAMING

seriously – to make sure this was what he wanted because there was no turning back once we said, "I Do!"

Likewise, successful people don't just let life happen to them. They proactively pursue their purpose by declaring their desires well ahead of them actually coming into existence. Terri Savelle Foy often says, "How you frame your words will be how you frame your world." Everything we've accomplished or failed to accomplish in our lives is because of us. It is easy to blame our parents, our environments, and even that employer who didn't grant us that well-deserved promotion. I know that isn't what most of us want to hear, but it is the truth. The person you see in the mirror is totally and completely responsible for where you are in life today. The good news, though, is that you don't have to stay there. Since words create your reality, you can change your words to create the life and relationship you want for "death and life are in the power of the tongue" (Prov 18:21a, KJV). While you may not be able to control the circumstances in your life, you can control how you respond to those circumstances. Chances

## My Marriage, My D.E.S.T.I.N.Y.

are that you dreamed of all the possibilities at the beginning of your relationship, but they were lost somewhere along the way. In fact, most people never see their dreams come to pass because they get it all wrong. They either never get started, or they never write their dreams down and revisit them!

Creating an affirmation statement is a tool to keep your dreams in front of you because you actually believe yourself better than you believe anyone else. And what you repeatedly hear, you eventually believe. Your affirmation statement should be short and succinct but specific. You should also state your affirmation statement in the present tense, and it should invoke a positive emotion. Finally, you should ensure the statement is readily accessible and reviewed often (at least 2-3 times a day—morning, noon, and night). You can keep copies of your affirmation on your phone, desktop computer, bathroom or anywhere else you visit frequently. Bottom line—it is important to review your dreams regularly so it is easier to visualize your desired life as if it is already achieved.

## DREAMING

This all begins with the outlook you desire to have about your marriage. Develop a mindset of being in it to win it which starts with a lifelong commitment...a lifelong dream! Be sure to express yourself and understand that your significant other is not able to read your mind. It is also important to know that everything you do or fail to do affects your mate. If one of you or both of you choose not to live a healthy lifestyle, both of you will eventually suffer the consequences. Fortunately or unfortunately, these decisions will impact your lives for many years to come. When we're younger, we tend to think we're invincible. These seemingly trivial decisions won't make that big of a difference, or will they? Of course they will! Daily, seemingly insignificant actions will result in major strides toward your goals.

It is imperative to share your dreams with your significant other, so you're both on the same page for supporting each other. Dreaming creates a mindset that makes couples more forward-thinking, which can help them focus on something other than the daily annoyances that the best of relationships contend with. These

## My Marriage, My D.E.S.T.I.N.Y.

annoyances can fall anywhere from one preferring to fall asleep to music while the other needs silence—to one never cleaning up after themselves while the other has borderline OCD (obsessive-compulsive disorder), and the list goes on. Vision gives your relationship direction to move toward your goals like a GPS (global positioning system) Tracker. Consequently, couples tend to drift apart if they do not have a shared vision. The changes may be subtle over time until you wake up one day and wonder why you no longer want to spend the rest of your days with the person sleeping beside you.

Raising children may create added challenges during their various stages of development, and you will likely have less disposable time and money. Believe it or not, they actually grow up and will eventually leave home one day—maybe even sooner than you think. If you fail to make your marriage a priority, what should be the time of you and your lover's lives ends up being one where you decide to part ways. You didn't even realize you were gradually drifting apart until you became strangers over the years and no longer recognized each other. Keep hope alive

## DREAMING

because this can be prevented! Your children are watching your example and will benefit greatly from your healthy relationship.

After you've started your family, raised the kiddos, solidified your careers and purchased a home, you want to challenge each other to keep learning about one another, growing together and communicating changes in expectations and deeds that evolve over time. Everything changes over time for better or for worse. There are some factors that can minimize the impact of these changes. Particularly, it helps if the two of you are at least headed in the same direction spiritually, emotionally and financially at a minimum. A mentor and a community of like-minded couples help promote a positive environment and a stronger relationship bond.

One of our personal, life-long goals was military retirement. It was all we knew, where we spent most of our adult lives together and, geographically, where we raised our children. We supported each other during peacetime and wartime, highs and lows, and so many ups and downs. Together, we managed to survive and

## My Marriage, My D.E.S.T.I.N.Y.

thrive through it all. The problem was we didn't adjust those goals, and once we completed this milestone, everything around us seemed to crumble. Problems will come and problems will go, but when you focus on your dreams instead of despair, your outlook is far greater. After all, *"obstacles are what you see when you take your eyes off your goals"* (Vince Lombardi). I don't want you to make that same mistake, so please do not forget to adjust your dreams and create new ones as they are checked off your list.

Make the commitment to love each other no matter what you may confront. Dream of growing old together, but don't forget to enjoy today before it's too late. Paul and Vickie have been married for over 37 years. They understand the importance of dreaming together. Among other things, they eagerly anticipate the day they are both retired, so they can freely visit the retirement home they're constructing in Ghana, West Africa. They also have plans to use some of their land as a base to educate the less fortunate in their home state of Arkansas. Their lives have been centered on serving, and this is something that began with a

## DREAMING

thought – a dream – that they eventually put in the work to make a reality. What a wonderful opportunity to give back—as a couple sharing a dream!

While it is important to dream, "a dream without a plan is nothing more than a wish."[iii] The time to stop watching others live their dreams and start living yours is NOW. Get off of the sidelines and get in the game to make your latter years better than your former ones. We can't change the past, but there is no need to silently envy the success of others when you can create your own success. CS Lewis once said, "You are never too old to set another goal or to dream a new dream," so never lose touch with your future! Keep your dreams a priority and at the forefront of your mind and your relationship. This keeps you progressing and anticipating something better, but you must first identify your own desires.

"Dream your life, and then live your dreams. Each person's DESTINY is not a matter of chance, it's a matter of choice. It's determined by what we say, what we do and whom we

## My Marriage, My D.E.S.T.I.N.Y.

trust." (Truett Cathy - Founder, Chick-fil-A). While you're at it don't forget to honor and support each other's individual dreams which require you to do some personal soul-searching and involve vulnerability with your life-long partner. Sharing dreams, encouraging one another along the way and celebrating each other's successes seals your bond and helps you to believe in each other. We must always respect the similarities and even the differences of each other's dreams. Whatever you do, NEVER STOP DREAMING!

## DREAMING

**Personal Application**

1. Set a timer and make an individual list of at least 20-50 things you would like to accomplish in your lifetime if you had no limitations. (e.g., it can be as simple as paying off ALL debt, taking a dream vacation, or meeting a famous person).

_____

_____

_____

_____

_____

_____

_____

_____

_____

My Marriage, My D.E.S.T.I.N.Y.

2. Once each of you has made your list, review it together for commonality and prioritize what you want to accomplish first by compiling at least 10 dreams you can pursue together. This will be a critical step unless you're the exception with unlimited resources. Settle any differences in an amicable manner for you have a lifetime to get it all done!

_____

_____

_____

_____

_____

_____

## DREAMING

3. Create a dream affirmation statement and review it regularly as a couple. You can find guidelines and an example on the free resources page at crowningdestinies.com.

## Chapter 3: EMPATHY

*People may forget what you said, but they will never forget how you made them feel.*

MAYA ANGELOU
American Poet and Activist

Empathy is one of those things that's hard to describe, but you just know when it is there...or not. Understanding empathy as it relates to your relationship is crucial to building a lifelong legacy. We all have a deep, innermost need to feel love and connection, and a major purpose of our existence is to meet each other's needs. That is, to selflessly serve one another without necessarily seeking something in return. Empathy promotes an in-depth connection to your spouse and is the gateway to filling that need.

It is important to clarify some truths regarding empathy that are often confused with sympathy. Although the terms are similar, they are not

## EMPATHY

interchangeable. Whereas you understand the other person's feelings and offer your assistance, perhaps, with some emotional distance in sympathy, empathy lends a deeper care and concern for what the person is dealing with. In its simplest form, empathy is being considerate and sensitive to others' emotions. It is also free of judgment while acknowledging their position in a given situation. Keep in mind that "if you judge people, you have no time to love them." (Mother Teresa) The ultimate goal of empathy is to connect and improve or share the other person's mood after they have shared a meaningful concern with you.

Say your wife is pouring her heart out about a problem she's having at work. You briskly tell her you're sorry and immediately turn away to continue watching your favorite show on Netflix. She would not feel you were sincere despite your sympathy efforts. Empathy, on the other hand, would cause you to give your wife your undivided attention while she shares her concern with you, and maybe even give her a hug and a word of encouragement to show you can relate to what she's dealing with. Empathy

My Marriage, My D.E.S.T.I.N.Y.

requires compassion and heartfelt understanding. It requires you to place yourself in your spouse's shoes and feel what they're feeling. It requires you to identify the emotion they're experiencing, whether it is happiness, sadness, frustration or joy—and then validating those feelings before offering a solution. This does not mean you have to agree with how they're feeling or what they're sharing.

Sometimes either of you may just want a listening ear and other times you may want help solving your dilemma. Many men's natural response is to want to solve the problem, whereas women often just want a listening ear...at least initially. Effective communication is necessary to know the appropriate response to use at any given time. Don't forget to maintain eye contact to show you're concerned and focused on what is being shared. After twenty-five years of marriage, Anthony and Renetta continue to hold "connection sessions" to ensure they are still meeting each other's needs. They avoid making assumptions and seek direct feedback to assess their ever-changing lives. It has been a constant learning

# EMPATHY

and evolving scenario for both. Empathy requires a level of vulnerability and surrender to your mate, which intensifies the connection when you can relate to some extent. It "...is like giving someone a psychological hug." (Lawrence J. Bookbinder)

Nurse scholar, Theresa Wiseman, studied empathy which resulted in four defining attributes: See the world as others see it, understand without having to agree, understand another's feelings then, now, and later, and then communicate the understanding so it can be felt (PhD, PGDEd, BSc(Hons)Psych, RGN, RNCT).

Empathy and communication go hand in hand in an intimate relationship but are sources of contention for many couples. Generally speaking, a lot of women tend to "talk" more than most men. It turns out that a Stanford study shows the hippocampus in a woman is actually larger than a man's which may offer a scientific explanation for this genetic difference. The hippocampus is responsible for how information is processed in the brain.

## My Marriage, My D.E.S.T.I.N.Y.

Both verbal and nonverbal communication provide meaningful feedback. Verbal communication is how you speak, the tone in your voice, and how you inflect and deflect your voice. I'm sure you've heard someone say, "It's not what you said but how you said it," and that applies whether it was positive or negative. Nonverbal communication is anything not spoken—from the way you dress, your posture, eye contact, and most importantly in relationships, your facial gestures.

Active listening involves verbal and nonverbal communication and is vital in the couple's communication loop, especially during conflict. When you actively listen, you are not constructing your response while your spouse is talking. Instead, you give them your full attention to ensure you thoroughly understand their concerns. This may include repeating what you thought you heard your spouse say, but this process builds trust and connection. Actively listening to each other is nothing more than being open enough to compassionately give your spouse your attentiveness and sincerely addressing their concerns.

# EMPATHY

Feel what they feel and know what they need, so you don't end up in a situation where you're sacrificing and thinking you're giving them everything. You could be giving them everything except the very thing they want and need. Gary Chapman's book, *The 5 Love Languages*[iv], is a valuable resource to ensure you are speaking your partner's language. The five, self-explanatory love languages are: Words of Affirmation, Quality Time, Receiving Gifts, Acts of Service, and Physical Touch. One discovery I made about the 5 love languages is that your primary love language can change over time. I see it as reflecting your needs during the different seasons of your life. Clearly, a woman's language being "acts of service" will peak higher on the charts when the babies are younger and more demanding. You can access the quiz to determine your love language and other useful information on the free resources page at crowningdestinies.com.

Earlier in our relationship, I found communicating sensitive issues in writing to be more effective...especially if we were both passionate about a particular topic. Russ and I

## My Marriage, My D.E.S.T.I.N.Y.

both have fairly strong personalities, and we just found this method of communication to be more effective since it allowed both of us to get our uninterrupted thoughts out while having the time to think it through and package it in such a way that it was less offensive to the other. This was also useful for clarifying what was actually stated rather than fueling a misinterpretation. Once we released our deepest concerns in written form, we would come together to close the loop on any lingering concerns. Overall, this was a way to help us diffuse conflict, but you need to also be aware of a few others.

Take care not to get caught up in showing empathy to the opposite sex. Believe it or not most affairs did not enter the "friendship" stage with a plan for things to go the wrong way. If you establish boundaries early on, you'll never have to undo what was never done. I heard a pastor once say he looks "up, up, and away" when dealing with the opposite sex to avoid potential problems.

Watch your words for your mouth speaks from the abundance of your heart. Take a moment

## EMPATHY

to collect your thoughts before using words you might later regret. Take deep, slow breaths to get centered. Always strive to get your heart and mind synchronized in order to reach a heart-centered approach and response because transformation begins in the heart.

Empathy requires a mindset of being in it to win it. When you're emotionally disconnected, sexual disconnection typically follows and can negatively impact other areas of the relationship. However, when there is an emotional connection, both are more responsive and will benefit in every other area including sexual intimacy. These heart connections can lead to greater sexual fulfillment, but we'll discuss that more later on. There are no perfect marriages anywhere, but two imperfect beings joining forces to do life together and deciding to overlook the other's daily annoyances. "When you stop expecting people to be perfect, you can like them for who they are." (Donald Miller) Things are not always as they seem, so avoid comparing yourself to what others seem to be, do and have in their relationships. People only allow you to see what they want you to see,

## My Marriage, My D.E.S.T.I.N.Y.

which is important to note when viewing social media posts.

If maintaining a long-term, intimate relationship is your desire, you have to develop a compassionate heart of empathy. While empathy allows you to understand your spouse and create a connection of the soul, it is also important to know yourself on an intimate level.

# EMPATHY

## Personal Application

1. Ask your significant other to rate your role as husband/wife on a scale of 1 to 10 (with 1 being low and 10 being high) over the past (week, month, etc.). If you're rated at anything less than a 10, try not to get angry and start defending yourself (which is a natural response initially). Instead, ask what actions you could specifically take to increase your score to a 10.

_____

_____

_____

_____

_____

_____

_____

My Marriage, My D.E.S.T.I.N.Y.

2. In an effort to listen with greater empathy, ask your spouse how their day was or the status of an important project they're pursuing. Practice listening attentively without interrupting, without judging and always assessing their nonverbal communication. This is a great opportunity to connect emotionally, but it will certainly take practice for mastery.

_____

_____

_____

_____

_____

_____

_____

## EMPATHY

3. Ask your mate what lights them up and makes them feel loved. Then, seek an opportunity, to apply what they shared with you when they least expect it.

_____

_____

_____

_____

_____

_____

_____

_____

My Marriage, My D.E.S.T.I.N.Y.

# Chapter 4: SELF-AWARENESS

*We cannot change what we are not aware of, and once we are aware, we cannot help but change.*

SHERYL SANDBERG
Chief Operating Officer, Facebook

Many of us go our entire lives without ever becoming self-aware. That is, we never learn who we are at the core. Self-awareness requires a level of maturity that allows us to take a more inward assessment than an outward one. There are two types of self-awareness—internal and external. Internal self-awareness is our capacity to take a step back and evaluate our thoughts, our beliefs, our values, our past and even our future actions, which help us understand what shapes us and makes us uniquely who we are. External self-awareness is understanding how we are perceived by others and what they think of us. The two are typically incongruent, and it is not uncommon for

## SELF-AWARENESS

others to think more highly of us than we think of our own, critical selves.

Self-awareness helps you accept your strengths and limitations without being judgmental of yourself and others. Your perception ultimately becomes your reality, and your very thoughts, beliefs and values define you as a person. While you need to be honest with yourself, you also need to demonstrate self-compassion and be loving and accepting of your flaws. That's not to say you shouldn't seek self-improvement. You just need to be okay with the things you can't change, such as the shade of your skin, or the things you choose not to change, such as your core beliefs. Fully embrace the opportunity and benefits of accepting and harmonizing with yourself.

Self-awareness is also a critical tool to reach your highest, most fulfilling self. Although everyone is not great at everything, everyone is great at something. And each of us is uniquely designed with our own set of strengths, gifts and talents. Albert Einstein once said "...if you judge a fish by its ability to climb a tree, it will live its whole life believing that it is stupid." We need to maximize our unique abilities rather than dwell on our weaknesses, not to be mistaken with tackling and mastering a new skill.

Most people respond better to positive reinforcement, and you are no different. Be gentle with yourself if you make a mistake. Absolutely every human makes mistakes, but you must be able to forgive yourself, learn from the experience, and move on. I consider myself a recovering perfectionist. Realizing I was not perfect and that everyone makes mistakes was one of the greatest gifts I could receive. Of course, we always want to seek improvement, but as long as we're breathing, we'll never achieve the status of perfection—neither as an individual nor in our relationships. That was an incredibly liberating enlightenment for me after spending most of my life with the former mindset. Intentional focus on abundance and practicing gratitude for what I had instead of what I did not, also tremendously helped me progress in this area. When you are grateful, you attract more things to be grateful for. Learning to appreciate YOU for YOU is when

## SELF-AWARENESS

you become aware of your true worth. Then, you are better equipped to pour into your relationship. You'll be able to not only accept but also appreciate your personality differences without fear of losing your own identity. This also helps you become more aware and sensitive to conflict triggers. Consequently, you can cope with anger management better since you'll better understand the causes, differences, and responses as a result of your own interpretations rather than the intended purpose.

We often make ourselves the lowest priority until the point that we're completely depleted and have nothing else to give to anyone else, let alone ourselves. Just as you have to place your own oxygen mask on before assisting others with theirs, you must also take care of yourself before you can offer anything of value to your spouse—or anyone else for that matter. When you are self-aware, you recognize the importance of self-care before you can give yourself fully to your significant other.

## My Marriage, My D.E.S.T.I.N.Y.

Knowing ourselves intimately enables us to build stronger relationships. Two halves certainly do not make a whole when it comes to having a fulfilling relationship. Instead, it takes two whole, self-aware beings to create a whole, thriving relationship. Otherwise, you may have another set of issues to confront. To be self-aware enough to give of yourself completely in your relationship, at some point you must identify any gaps in the relationship and commit to doing something about it.

Generally speaking, women are no longer as financially and physically dependent on men as they once were. Nonetheless, we still "need" them in other areas of our lives to make us feel wanted and needed despite our independence and self-awareness. This does not mean we lose our individuality in the process. I like to think of it as *my man accentuates my life*, but it all starts with being whole within myself. Once you become aware of where you stand, you can recreate your desired outcome. After all, if you don't know who you are and what you want, how can you relay those desires to your mate or expect them to figure it out? Basically, we

## SELF-AWARENESS

should be interdependent with each other rather than being helplessly and hopelessly dependent beings.

We need to be self-aware because we can't control the actions of others. However, we can control how we respond to them. So, before you expect your spouse to make you happy, take a moment to reevaluate your circumstances because YOU are the only one who can make YOU happy in the long run. Never depend on anyone else for your happiness. That is a terrible responsibility to impose on someone who isn't aware of all the emotional baggage, expectations and innermost heart's desires you bring to the relationship. Expectations that only you can meet, and your insecurities can spill over into the relationship and cause unnecessary issues.

You should be able to be yourself without pretending to be someone or something you're not. That's why it helps to establish a friendship with your mate and accept them the way they are rather than how you want them to be. Then, you need to communicate clearly what you're

## My Marriage, My D.E.S.T.I.N.Y.

seeking. Accordingly, you need to accept your mate for who they are. In many cases we know they need some tweaking before we say, "I do," but we assume we'll convert them into the exact mold we're seeking as time progresses. Focus on fixing YOU, and everything else will fall in place. The way you feel about yourself can even affect the intimacy in your relationship and cause your bedroom experience to suffer.

Embrace self-love, respect and acceptance while avoiding self-rejection and judgment! Love begins with loving yourself. Be present with yourself. Loved ones may overlook and even resist the positive changes you're making initially, but it will eventually trigger them to reconsider their own life choices. They may become uncomfortable with their current way of doing things and feel challenged to change their own lives. I think women, especially, underestimate their power and influence. The saying that a happy wife yields a happy life speaks volumes to this. Together with our spouses, we shape and mold our children to work towards their destinies. We set the atmosphere and tone within our homes, and we

## SELF-AWARENESS

are the first round of experience to show our children what marriage is all about.

Just as we benefit from a personal growth plan to continue growing and developing into a better version of ourselves every day, growing together in marriage is necessary for a lasting, happy, successful, and healthy marriage. The plan should allow for change and growth as individuals as well as evolving expectations and expressions of love. A great relationship needs to not only appreciate the similarities but also respect the differences in how the other views the world. Mutual interdependence enables a deep connection to one another.

Self-awareness and an abundance mindset foster total peace and fulfillment in every area of your life. Each and every one of us is predestined with an expected end, but we must first master ourselves before we can add value to our other relationships. Lifelong love doesn't just happen. It is the result of intentional action. Without first knowing and loving yourself, it can be difficult to love and be happy with anyone else.

## My Marriage, My D.E.S.T.I.N.Y.

Always be aware of the impact of your thoughts and words about yourself and your spouse...even when they can't hear you.

Everything begins with a thought, and people think according to what's in their hearts. Speak life into your relationship. Think about the influence you and your relationship have on each other, on your children, and on your family as a whole. You can fool some of the people some of the time, but you can't fool all of the people all of the time. One group of people you surely can't fool is your children and extended family members. I was deeply moved by my daughter Rashelle's observation of my relationship with her dad now that she has been introduced to the dating world. She felt that we were best friends, respected each other, enjoyed one another's company and loved each other passionately. Out of curiosity, I decided to ask my baby girl, Rashon, about her perception of our relationship. She said she admired how we respect each other, support each other's goals, and how we're always doing little things to make each other feel special. How gratifying it is to know we've been a positive example of love without even realizing it, and I couldn't have

## SELF-AWARENESS

said it any better myself. Our children are watching everything we say and do. Today is a good day to be more intentional about creating this legacy for your family today.

My Marriage, My D.E.S.T.I.N.Y.

**Personal Application**

1. On a scale of 1-10 (1 being low, 10 being high), how would you rate your current level of self-awareness?

   _____

   _____

   _____

   _____

2. Based on the factors shared in this chapter, what can you do to improve your own self-awareness. And how will this awareness improve your relationship?

   _____

   _____

   _____

   _____

## SELF-AWARENESS

3. What are a couple of limitations you have that your significant other can assist you with? Share them with each other.

_____

_____

_____

_____

_____

_____

_____

_____

_____

My Marriage, My D.E.S.T.I.N.Y.

# Chapter 5: THANKFULNESS

*Be thankful for what you have; you'll end up having more. If you concentrate on what you don't, you will never, ever have enough.*

OPRAH WINFREY
Actor, Philanthropist, and All-Time Queen of Talk Show Television

One of our deepest human needs is to feel appreciated. Various studies support this premise. Yet, we have entirely too many ungrateful people in the world—people who concentrate more on what they lack rather than their many blessings. They want to feel appreciated but often miss out due to their negative focus. Having an abundance mentality promotes giving rather than a scarcity mindset that causes one to keep everything to themselves. Thinking abundantly proves to be a valuable attribute in relationships. When you make a conscious effort to celebrate your spouse's achievements as well as the things you enjoy, great or small, you will inherently

## THANKFULNESS

create more opportunities for enjoyment. Expressing your gratitude can come in the form of verbal praise or affirmation as well as a tangible gift.

An attitude of gratitude shifts the entire atmosphere. It is often stated that it's difficult to be angry and grateful at the same time. Expressing gratitude brings tremendous benefits to a relationship such as enhancing connection and reducing stress and tension. We love to share the positive things in our life, so those we care most about will celebrate with us. Think about when you were first engaged to be married—you couldn't wait to tell the world, your best friend, your mom or even share it on your social media platform. I still call my mom today to share my greatest joys, and my girls are always eager to share their accomplishments with Russ and me, whether they mastered an exam at school or received any other special recognition.

If you want to reinforce any behavioral outcome, you must express gratitude. Russ and I may not always get it right, but we make every effort to

## My Marriage, My D.E.S.T.I.N.Y.

appreciate each other. It is so easy to take for granted all the little day-to-day activities that keep the homefront running smoothly. I am often reminded of just how well Russ takes care of us...when he's away, and I have to fend for myself!

When we lived in the National Capital Region, I totally minimized how Russ would shovel snow from our porch and driveway because he never uttered a mumbling word. During this particular time he was away on an untimely business trip. In a perfect world we would have been able to stay home during these arctic conditions, but this was an important day that my daughter, Rashelle, had been eagerly awaiting for quite some time. It was the day for her to take the test that would bring her only one step away from black belt status in Tae Kwon Do. While I was getting Rashelle and Rashon dressed, some teenage boys from the neighborhood were going door to door offering to shovel the main pathways for a small fee. Being the frugal person I am, I turned it down thinking I could easily take care of it myself. Boy, was I in for a surprise! That remains one of the most

## THANKFULNESS

physically demanding things I've had to do yet! And did I mention that it was below zero? I had a lot of thanking to do for every single one of Russ' previous shoveling efforts, and that gift didn't cost me a dime.

Do what you do for your spouse because you want to do it and because you enjoy doing it, not because you expect something in return or feel a sense of obligation. Your attitude deeply influences how your gratitude is perceived and received. Another way to show your spouse you appreciate them is to encourage a guys' or girls' night out. It shows you trust them even when they're not physically in your presence. While having brief times apart promotes keeping your own identity in sight, too much time apart can have a detrimental effect on your marriage without the proper tools.

The least expensive, yet extremely valuable gift you can give your spouse is to affirm them with your words. You want to edify them with your words daily because people fall in love with you because of how they feel about themselves when they are with you. What a great way to fall

My Marriage, My D.E.S.T.I.N.Y.

in love over and over again. Yet, there are so many who choose to tear their spouses down and even publicly scold or challenge them. Let me caution you to avoid this approach at all costs as it is a great way to place your relationship on the road to destruction. Remember, the power of life and death is in your tongue. Choose today to give your relationship life.

Just as there's a language barrier between a person who speaks only English and one who only speaks Spanish, the same holds true if a couple isn't communicating according to the other's love language. Thank your spouse in accordance with their love language. An effective way to show thanks is by giving according to your spouse's needs and desires. I mentioned earlier that *The 5 Love Languages* book discusses various love languages to connect with your spouse. Learning these languages has had a significant impact on our relationship and allows us to serve one another according to the other's inherent needs.

## THANKFULNESS

We are on the same team as our spouse, not in competition with one another. As you might suspect, speaking ill-will toward your spouse never strengthens the team. In fact, competition lends room for unnecessary conflict.

Teammates should build each other up with support and encouragement rather than tearing each other down. Remember to celebrate what you want to see more of.

The greatest gift you can give the love of your life is the gift of your unconditional love. Love is an action word, and it is imperative that you express your love outwardly according to your mate's love language, whether it is with words of affirmation or a bouquet of flowers. Bottom line—what makes someone feel appreciated obviously means different things for different people.

I discovered just how ungrateful I was when I started being more intentional about my gratitude. The more gratitude you express, the more abundance you experience, and the more

My Marriage, My D.E.S.T.I.N.Y.

abundance you experience, the more fulfilling your relationship is.

## THANKFULNESS

**Personal Application**

1. Identify you and your spouse's primary love languages and take deliberate actions to speak them accordingly. You can find useful tools on the free resources page at crowningdestinies.com.

My Marriage, My D.E.S.T.I.N.Y.

2. Start a gratitude journal capturing at least one thing you are grateful for with your spouse each day for a set period of time (e.g., one week or one month). It may be more difficult to seek out these things initially, but it gets easier and will be so worth it as you get used to "hunting the positive."

_____

_____

_____

_____

_____

_____

_____

_____

## THANKFULNESS

3. Be intentional and refrain from murmuring or complaining about anything negative for a full day. Instead, be a breath of positive fresh air.

_____

_____

_____

_____

_____

_____

_____

_____

My Marriage, My D.E.S.T.I.N.Y.

# Chapter 6: INTEGRITY

*The glue that holds all relationships together... is trust, and trust is based on integrity.*

BRIAN TRACY
Motivational Speaker and Self-Development Author

Integrity or trust is the foundation of marriage. Consequently, relationships are unstable without it. Trust is one of those touchy subjects that is built one step at a time over a given period, but it only takes missing one step to take you all the way back to the bottom. It is established from common interests and consistent dependability. Though it is sometimes difficult to achieve, trust can magnify and deepen a relationship greatly over time. On the other hand, an inability to have faith and confidence in your spouse can cause your relationship to suffer greatly. After all, your word is your bond. So, what's love without trust?

## INTEGRITY

Many couples have had to confront trust issues over the life of their relationships. Once trust is broken, rebuilding it can be an arduous task. One of the most challenging to overcome is infidelity. According to the American Association for Marriage and Family Therapy, national surveys indicate about 35 percent of women and 45 percent of men have engaged in extramarital affairs - whether the affair was sexual or just emotional.

It is important to have systems in place to protect the integrity of your marriage and establish boundaries long before you actually need to. Love requires you to be vulnerable. One way to demonstrate trust and reassure one another is to share your passwords for your handheld devices and social media accounts. Some may say I don't have to prove myself if you trust me. Accountability locks in a system to help you avoid diver's temptations. We used to say in the military that it's not about trust, it's about accountability. If you already feel a need to hide encounters from your spouse, you're likely already having an emotional affair or have at least crossed that invisible line. The bottom

## My Marriage, My D.E.S.T.I.N.Y.

line is that it is inappropriate, unacceptable and has trouble written all over it!

Make your spouse a priority and create an environment to feel safe enough to share anything with them. You can also make it a habit to save sharing your greatest concerns, frustrations and joys with your mate before sharing them with anyone else! Likewise, withholding serious information to supposedly "protect your spouse" actually creates emotional distance in the relationship. Strive to make each other feel safe and maximize every connection opportunity you can.

We all go through hard things at some point in our marriages. It's important to get to the root of the problem so your focus is not merely on the issue or symptoms of the problem. We mentioned that infidelity is one of the most difficult challenges to overcome in a marriage. Yet, many focus on the betrayal itself rather than the root cause. It's imperative to address your concerns to allow for resolution.

Likewise, everyone does not apologize the

## INTEGRITY

same way. It's important to apologize in such a way that your spouse feels you are sincere. You have to remain flexible because what works in one instance may not necessarily work in another. This is where empathy and openly communicating with each other comes in. For some, a sincere verbal apology may work while others may need to see a tear fall to be convinced you're sincere. Still others may need to hear every detail of the offense before forgiving.

Rebuilding trust begins with the offender acknowledging their faults, identifying and discussing the root cause of the offense, and being sensitive to the victim's feelings and response to the situation. At the end of the day, action speaks louder than words and consistency brings about confidence. So, make sure your actions are in alignment with your words. Nonetheless, we all have choices in life. If you feel your mate is sincere, and you decide to forgive them, you need to be willing to let it go and not relive the heartache over and over again. We must also understand that everyone

## My Marriage, My D.E.S.T.I.N.Y.

has different levels of tolerance and willingness to forgive.

Once the victim feels the apology is sincere, they can decide whether or not to forgive. If you decide to forgive your spouse, you need to agree not to bring up the offense again. You will never be able to move forward by constantly revisiting the issue. This is not to say you will not need adequate time to fully heal or overcome the situation. It could take days, months or even years to become fully vulnerable again. Nonetheless, forgiveness should wipe the slate squeaky clean, so you can begin the rebuilding process. It can be difficult to rebuild trust once it has been violated, and counseling may be crucial to the healing process. Either way, forgiveness is necessary.

It is also important to understand that not everyone apologizes the same way. You have some who simply act as if nothing ever happened while another may just verbally apologize. Still others may present a gift as a sacrifice for their apology. It is crucial that you meet your mate's apology expectations to make

## INTEGRITY

it easier for them to forgive you. This is one area you must note the crucial role of open communication.

It took me a number of years to finally learn that my husband really could not read my mind. Imagine that. I intentionally held back from sharing some of my deepest concerns because I falsely felt it was his duty to "discover" my innermost needs and desires. I'll bet you've experienced something similar in your own relationship or know someone who has. My husband is a wonderful man but, unfortunately, he was not blessed with the gift of mindreading. I guess we'll have to work on that.

On a serious note, communication is not a game of chance, so please remember to share your thoughts, concerns and frustrations with your spouse. It is indeed the bridge that will unite the two of you and bring you closer to one another. Many couples wait years before seeking help, and things are sometimes too far gone once they finally seek resolution.

## My Marriage, My D.E.S.T.I.N.Y.

A true test of integrity is refusing compromise, but let's say the human side of us kicks in and makes a mistake. The right thing to do is to forgive. I know that some offenses are more difficult to overcome than others, and you may consider them unforgivable. Understand that forgiveness is actually for you more than it is for them. And if you're the offender, you must first learn to forgive yourself. Once you can forgive yourself, the healing process can begin. Your perception is your reality, but love covers a multitude of sins.

Is willfully withholding some of the facts a breach of integrity? Spicie and Laron had to overcome an integrity compromise early in their marriage. Laron consciously withheld that he had actually been married and divorced more times than he revealed to Spicie while they were dating. Unfortunately, Spicie did not learn the truth until after they were already married! It was not easy for her to come to grips with this, but she was eventually able to forgive Laron. It is highly likely that she would not have given him a chance had she known the truth earlier in the dating process. Now, this certainly does not

## INTEGRITY

suggest taking the deceptive route because many relationships never overcome situations like this. Spicie and Laron can laugh about it today and have been happily married for twenty-two years now.

Watch your words (or lack of words) for they can hurt for a long time. A wound can heal but the scar remains. We can't change the past. "Yesterday is history. Tomorrow is a mystery." But "today is a gift. That's why it is called the present." (Eleanor Roosevelt) Forgiveness is never for the other person. It is a gift to you. Marianne Williamson once said that "unforgiveness is like drinking poison yourself and waiting for the other person to die." Forgiveness is liberating, and we are to bless, not curse, those who have hurt us. Let it Go! Whatever it is—you must forgive if you want to be forgiven of any wrongdoing in your past or present or future. It can be difficult to move past some pain and may take something greater than you to get through it.

So, why is it that you never hear a parent say they are putting their child up for adoption if they

## My Marriage, My D.E.S.T.I.N.Y.

are disobedient one more time? We love our children unconditionally—regardless of what they do or fail to do and regardless of what they say or fail to say. We need to have that same mindset and attitude about our relationships instead of walking around with one foot in the door and one foot out. Relationships get stronger when both of you are willing to understand mistakes and forgive each other; it is very important to attack the issues rather than each other. Avoid criticism!

I have never met a couple who said they shared dreams with their spouse, showed empathy, and appreciated and trusted their spouse while simultaneously engaging in an extramarital affair. In most instances, there was something "missing" in the relationship. In order to have a healthy relationship, the highest integrity and unwavering trust are essential elements. You want to have and sustain an unquestionable character, morals and values. Be very conscious about your words and your deeds for they become your reality. Integrity is taking the hard right (honesty) over the easy wrong (betrayal) whether or not anyone else is aware

## INTEGRITY

of your actions. When necessary, choose to forgive, and give your relationship a new start to have a fighting chance at leaving a legacy.

My Marriage, My D.E.S.T.I.N.Y.

**Personal Application**

1. If there is an unresolved breach in integrity in your relationship, address it, forgive it and put it behind you, so your healing can begin. Seek counseling intervention if you're unable to resolve the matter.

_____

_____

_____

_____

2. Share your thoughts on why maintaining an integrous relationship is important.

_____

_____

_____

_____

## INTEGRITY

3. What are some specific ways you can fool-proof the integrity in your relationship?

My Marriage, My D.E.S.T.I.N.Y.

# Chapter 7: NEWNESS

*The secret of change is to focus all of your energy not on fighting the old, but on building the new.*

SOCRATES
Greek Philosopher

Who doesn't like new things? I can't think of anyone, and that includes the young as well as the old. Think about how that new dress or suit feels against your skin when you wear it for the first time. I'll bet you walk around with your head held a little higher and your smile a little wider. It makes you feel brand new, refreshed, and rejuvenated. The same philosophy holds true in your relationship. Always be willing to try something new to keep things "spicy" because life can easily get boring and mundane after doing things the same way at the same old time, day after day.

Many couples lose interest in each other because they either start arguing over trivial

## NEWNESS

tasks, or they just start taking life too seriously. Think back to when you first started dating. You had the excitement of discovering all about one another at your fingertips, but what happened once you thought you had it all figured out? I'll tell you what happens if you're like most couples in the world. It is so easy to get complacent, think you know everything, and start taking each other for granted. This doesn't necessarily happen intentionally, but you may gradually begin prioritizing everything else over your mate. And before you know it, you get caught up in the routine of rushing to and from work, helping the kids with homework, and preparing dinner over and over.

Let's face it, children demand our attention greatly at different stages of their lives. Add in wearing a nine to five hat where you must excel in order to climb the corporate ladder and keep the bills paid. No wonder priorities shift during this season of life. Even so, it is not too late to turn things around and acquire the tools necessary to begin thriving or take your thriving to another level in your relationship. Having a coach or mentor is a way to get there quicker. I

## My Marriage, My D.E.S.T.I.N.Y.

have a coach in just about every important area of my life—from a business coach to a fitness coach and even a memory coach. You need this example from someone you respect and who you would be willing to trade places with to go farther faster.

Love is an action word, and NEW action is the seasoning necessary to add flavor to your relationship. One way to avoid boredom and break up the monotony is to schedule date nights.

Date nights allow you to be lighthearted and playful with intention. It allows you to let your hair down. Try not to take each other too seriously all of the time, and understand that there is a time and a place for everything. Learn the difference between when it's time to buckle down and get it done and when a lighthearted approach is more appropriate. Playfulness and just enjoying each other's company allow you to escape your usual hectic schedules and focus on reconnecting with one another. Russ and I love comedy and always look forward to attending live performances. We have also

## NEWNESS

enjoyed exploring new adventures over the years. Every day you awaken is a new day filled with opportunities to grow your love. Make date night a regularly scheduled priority on your calendar and try new things to keep it exhilarating.

Since relationships can sometimes lose their sizzle and can fizzle after you've been married for a while, integrating the surprise element is another way to keep things "spicy" and new. Despite the need for predictability, we also need challenges, and a few unknowns or a degree of uncertainty in our relationships. I know this may seem contradictory, but both are necessary to have a fulfilling relationship. "Variety is indeed the spice of life."

Just as everyone looks forward to the new year for another chance at getting things right, there are great benefits in keeping our relationships fresh. Small, seemingly insignificant improvements can have a huge impact on relationships. Maximize every opportunity to work toward making your new life exactly how you want it. Keeping things new and fresh is like

## My Marriage, My D.E.S.T.I.N.Y.

restarting, refreshing or rebooting. Restarting enables a new beginning. Refreshing provides new strength and energy or reinvigorates. Rebooting is usually necessary after a computer crashes, meaning it stops working because of a malfunction. Relationships sometimes crash or malfunction and need a reboot to get back to working normally.

Patti and Marocco take a vacation to a new location without their children each year. Most recently, they visited the Riviera. This practice allows them to anticipate their next vacation and instills the element of surprise to share a new experience together. They treasure the close friendship they've developed over the years and have been happily married for over twenty-four years now.

One area that can easily fall into complacency is your level of passion and intimacy. Although true love may hide at times, it never really dies. Many relationships go south or end because of a lack of intimacy. Intimacy falls into two major categories: physical and emotional. It creates a

## NEWNESS

level of closeness that makes you feel connected to your spouse. Many men gravitate towards physical intimacy while women display a greater need for emotional intimacy. Either way, couples typically don't divorce because they stop loving one another. They divorce because they have "fallen out of intimacy" with one another. Intimacy is the one thing that differentiates lovers from friends.

Some relationships suffer in the bedroom over time. Initially, both are eager to share in this beautiful display of love. After a while it can become a lesser priority for one or both partners. In most issues with sex in relationships, the root of the problem is not physical in nature. It is typically due to another unmet need, an emotional need. Again, I can't emphasize enough how important communication is to tackle these issues early on. To illustrate the power of the mind and the importance of meeting emotional needs, some women are able to bring themselves to orgasm by thought alone without any direct stimulation. A huge part of enjoying intimacy with your

## My Marriage, My D.E.S.T.I.N.Y.

spouse is learning to appreciate who you are and ultimately feeling good about yourself. The bedroom is not defiled, so whatever both of you are willing to do is permissible.

Men tend to be more visual, so let's keep things spicy by wearing that sexy lingerie, Ladies! Vernet and Lynette have learned to communicate this over the years. To ensure her emotional needs are met all day long, Lynette wears special lingerie early in the day to indicate her mood and expectations. She said it works every time, and Vernet gets right on board! They have been happily married for over twenty-two years.

Sexual intimacy is a beautiful thing to share with your spouse, but I think it goes without saying that some individuals enjoy it more frequently than others. It's important to understand that sexual intimacy is designed to bring each other pleasure. And in order to bring someone pleasure, a conversation is necessary to know what pleases them. You wouldn't just purchase a gift for someone without soliciting some suggestions from them, would you? Most of us

## NEWNESS

are constantly changing and often unaware of what it is we want ourselves. The same should hold true in your marriage. You stand a better chance of getting it right if you simply ASK. At any rate, I realize sex is an uncomfortable but important conversation to have if you want to get it right. Please know that most problems in the bedroom do not begin in the bedroom. They actually begin long before the sexual act itself. Tap into the emotional aspect of intimacy, and the physical will fall in place. I'm going to do my part and grab some pumps and a whip to spice things up and break up the monotony every so often (wink).

Avoid boredom and make your relationship predictably unpredictable, and always seek opportunities to try NEW things, visit NEW places and explore NEW opportunities. Your spouse's emotional needs will be met and result in greater physical fulfillment. What is something you don't normally do that can give your relationship a boost?

My Marriage, My D.E.S.T.I.N.Y.

**Personal Application**

1. Leave your spouse a hand-written love note or thoughtful message in a place they can't miss but wouldn't expect it (e.g., the car dash or a laptop bag).

   _____

   _____

   _____

   _____

2. Surprise your spouse with a gift you know they would enjoy on an occasion other than their birthday, Valentine's Day or Christmas. It should be thoughtful but does not have to be expensive.

   _____

   _____

   _____

## NEWNESS

3. Ask about your spouse's untapped sexual fantasies during your next date night. Construct a plan to see it through if both agree. Research the topic if necessary.

My Marriage, My D.E.S.T.I.N.Y.

# Chapter 8: YEARNING

*Love doesn't mean you will always agree, see eye to eye, or never have an argument. It means despite the bad days, you still can't see yourself without that person.*

Author Unknown

Love can present a roller coaster of emotions. Sometimes up and sometimes down. How can you possibly yearn for someone you don't want to be around because they work your last nerve? Of course, you cannot. That is why it is important to have the appropriate tools to promote the connection necessary for yearning.

If you have applied the aforementioned strategies from chapters two through seven, there should be no issue of you and your mate yearning for each other. I have yet to hear anyone say, "My spouse is meeting all of my needs. We dream together and show empathy. We're both self-aware, express how thankful we are to each other, trust each other and keep

## YEARNING

things new. I think I'll file for a divorce." That would be absurd, and it just doesn't happen when you make each other a priority and apply the key strategies. Rather, you will be overwhelmed by how satisfying and fulfilling your relationship is regardless of the number of years you've been married.

To yearn expresses the depth and passion desired for another. I want to highlight a couple of areas here for you to add to your toolkit. Greeting your love with a kiss enables connection and ignites the pleasure centers of the brain that encourage feelings of affection and bonding. According to research experts, kissing for at least ten seconds releases the oxytocin and dopamine hormones. Oxytocin is the same hormone secreted when breastfeeding your newborn. It is responsible for creating a connection and bond between mom and baby. This may explain why kissing creates intimate bonds. Dopamine triggers the same part of your brain that is stimulated and causes butterflies in your stomach.

Other studies show that kissing can reduce the

## My Marriage, My D.E.S.T.I.N.Y.

stress hormone, cortisol. This special kiss (what I call the connection kiss) will shift the atmosphere even without planning it that way. The only difference between your intimate relationship and your relationship with your friends is intimacy. If you find yourself in a situation where your relationship has died, you have no choice but to rebirth something new. That is—if you want to bring it back alive. Let's reignite the passion and keep the fire burning the way it used to be. Surely you want more than a platonic relationship or roommate!

To circle back, do you often long to be with the love of your life when you're apart? I once heard someone say you fall in love with someone because of how you feel about yourself when you're with that person. If you want to be longed for and desired, you need to assess the energy you're displaying. Nobody wants to be around someone who is negative, condescending or pessimistic all the time. Instead, strive to be affirming, uplifting and a ray of sunshine to your mate. And always be present when spending quality time together. That means your phone is put away, the television is turned off, and any

## YEARNING

other distractions you may have are eliminated. Who in their right mind would not long to be in the presence of this type of energy? I think it's safe to say: Nobody! Everyone wants to feel wanted and needed. And everyone wants to experience love and connection.

Keep your spouse a priority. Of course, it is fine to have your own circle of friends, but take care not to let them replace your mate. As previously mentioned, save those important moments of your day to share with your spouse first and foremost. This creates a connection that only the two of you share. Then, you can spill your beans with the rest of your crew or the other important people in your life.

The primary reason for forming a relationship is to meet a need, want or desire we can't meet ourselves. If you're going to make an effort to meet your partner's needs, it's important to understand what those needs are rather than acting on what you *think* they are. And even then it is crucial to communicate your needs and wants. Without this communication, feedback is

My Marriage, My D.E.S.T.I.N.Y.

lacking and left to assumptions. We've all heard where assumptions can lead you in any situation.

Bishop and Lady Reeves have been married for over forty-five years! What a testament to their relationship. Needless to say, they have experienced many life seasons together during that time, from health scares to watching their children and grandchildren blossom. Since Bishop was more introverted, and Ollie was more of an extrovert, he saw early on the importance of having time alone to sharpen his saw. They designated two important days out of each week: Mondays are their days alone which allows him time to decompress and stay grounded enough to pour more energy into Ollie on their dedicated day to spend all day together. They highly recommend having an experienced marriage mentor to consult with on this journey to increase the likelihood of standing the test of time.

Oftentimes, a spouse assumes they're giving their lover "everything." Rarely are they truly giving their spouse everything, rather, they're

## YEARNING

giving their spouse everything they think is needed or desired instead of getting direct feedback. The missing link is they failed to communicate what they actually needed. This feedback loop goes both ways. Just as the giver has the responsibility to seek feedback, the recipient also has the responsibility of providing feedback. That way neither of you end up in a situation where you're giving everything to your mate—everything except what they truly want or need. Sometimes, we may not even have a clue of what we want. It's also typically easier to express what you don't want. Do you know your innermost needs? Gary Chapman's, *Five Love Languages* is an awesome tool to discover your dominant love language, so you can meet your mate's needs with greater certainty. You still need to offer or provide continuous feedback to stay on track.

Even when you're apart due to a scheduled business trip or other commitments, intentionally make the other feel missed upon their return. Reassure them that things weren't quite the same without them. You could bring them a small gift as an expression of your love.

## My Marriage, My D.E.S.T.I.N.Y.

I heard one of my friends who travel often say she expects to receive some fresh flowers upon her return. Even a $10 or $20 bouquet from Walmart will do because it means a lot for her to feel her family missed her while she was away.

The very essence of our relationships exists, so we can meet each other's needs. Rarely will you see a one-sided relationship for an extended period. What typically happens is the positive behavior from one will inspire the other to reciprocate similar actions. If you happen to be in a difficult, one-sided relationship, I would give the situation at least six months to see if things start to turn around in your favor.

When we focus on meeting our mates' needs and loving them, connection and fulfillment occur. And when you have a fulfilling relationship, your presence and your absence should have significance to the other. You will yearn to spend the rest of your days with this person despite any disagreement because you love them unconditionally, and you are destined to be together. You are destined to be the generation set apart to be an example for

## YEARNING

others, an example for your children. You are destined to leave your marital legacy.

My Marriage, My D.E.S.T.I.N.Y.

## Personal Application

1. Avoid negativity and criticism of your spouse when addressing any concerns that will place most people on the defense. Instead, address your concerns and say how it makes you "feel" NOT what they "never" or "always" do. (e.g., I feel frustrated when you do not help me clean the house." instead of "You NEVER help me clean the house."

_____

_____

_____

_____

_____

_____

_____

## YEARNING

2. Incorporate a 10-second kiss with your spouse at least once a day. You could do it before parting for the day, just before bedtime, or any other convenient time.

   _____

   _____

   _____

3. What specific actions can you take (or eliminate) to encourage yearning in your relationship?

   _____

   _____

   _____

   _____

   _____

## Chapter 9: REFLECTIONS: The God Factor

*...When I found him whom my soul loves. I held him, and would not let him go...*

(Song of Solomon 3:4, ESV)

"Love is patient, love is kind. It does not envy, it does not boast, it is not proud. It does not dishonor others, it is not self-seeking, it is not easily angered, it keeps no record of wrongs. Love does not delight in evil but rejoices with the truth. It always protects, always trusts, always hopes, always perseveres. Love never fails..." (1 Cor 13:4-8a, NIV)

Russ and I have learned some valuable lessons from our own relationships as well as the experiences of others over several decades. And I get it. Bringing two totally different people together from two totally different backgrounds, with totally different expectations and outlooks on life can present challenges at its very core. You don't have to master every secret strategy

## REFLECTIONS: The God Factor

I introduced all at once to enjoy improvements, but if you commit to incrementally adding these practical strategies to your life, you will not be disappointed. Making consistent progress is the real reason we have fulfillment in our lives.

However, it takes something greater than self to stay "in love" considering our bodies' autonomic responses and the known and unknown influences from our childhoods. Though every couple mentioned throughout this book may not have "mastered" each D.E.ST.I.N.Y. strategy just yet, they all shared one common attribute of their successful marriages across the board. Each couple credited their relationship with God as the single most important reason for their relationship continuing to thrive for decades. This gave their relationships an unshakeable foundation, and their aspirations to please God are a critical deciding factor for why they're still together. Where the seven keys to leave a legacy of love symbolize every aspect of the home, God is the critical foundation each home must be built upon.

## My Marriage, My D.E.S.T.I.N.Y.

The couples put their faith and trust in God to rescue them from the many trials and tribulations they've experienced in their relationships over the years which allows them to love unconditionally—even when they don't feel like it. These couples say it was God who humbled them to be less self-centered, and focus on pleasing their spouses instead. "Do nothing out of selfish ambition or vain conceit. Rather, in humility value others above yourselves, not looking to your own interests but each of you to the interests of the others." (Philippians 2:3-5, NIV) It is far "easier" to please your spouse when pleasing God is a point of interest. And that is ultimately why we sought out our spouses and entered the relationships in the first place—to meet each other's needs. You know...fill in the gap.

Russ and I also share that commonality with these couples. Since the very early stages of our relationship, God has been at the center and an utmost priority. Despite some challenges along the way, it was God who softened our hearts to forgive even when our flesh wanted to be resentful and hold on to things, for "...love covers a multitude of sins." (1 Pet 4:8, NIV) Likewise, it was God who gave us opportunities when it sometimes felt like we were at the end of the road. It was God who showed up faithfully and gave us opportunities we didn't deserve. And it is God who keeps us faithful to one another when temptation is all around us. Our desire to please Him allows us to love each other even when we don't feel like it in our own might. For "with God ALL things are possible." (Matt 19:26, KJV)

I'm reminded of an African Proverb that says "if you want to go fast, go alone, (but) if you want to go far, go together" for together everyone achieves more. This is also applicable to your relationships since "a threefold cord is not quickly broken."

Ecclesiastes 4:9-12, says: "Two are better than one, because they have a good reward for their labor. For if they fall, one will lift up his companion. But woe to him who is alone when he falls, for he has no one to help him up. Again, if two lie down together, they will keep warm; but how can one be warm alone? Though one may

## My Marriage, My D.E.S.T.I.N.Y.

be overpowered by another, two can withstand him. And a threefold cord is not quickly broken."

I understand that everyone may not a believer. Whether or not you are a believer, God's principles and guidelines still work. There is no favoritism with him." (Eph 6:9, NIV) His Word says, "judge not, that ye be not judged." (Matt 7:1, KJV) And "he that is without sin...(should) cast a stone" (John 8:7, KJV) for ALL have sinned and come short. You do not have to be perfect to choose God's way of doing things, but "whatsoever good thing any man doeth, the same shall he receive of the Lord, whether he be bound or free." (Eph 6:8, KJV)

Marriage is a covenant with God and the foundation of the family. So, why do so many Christians fail to make love last forever? It is easy to take each other for granted and fail to appreciate what you have until you've already lost it forever. Unfortunately, it has been our culture to work on our marriages only when a problem exists which could increase the chances of it being at a point of no return. This

## REFLECTIONS: The God Factor

reactive approach allows things to get too far out of hand before giving it the time and attention it requires. We need to be more proactive in laying a solid foundation for our marriages, and consequently, our families.

I recently shared with my 79-year-old dad that I needed to give him a call back because Russ and I were going into our marriage meeting. His response was, "What's wrong with you and Russ?" The hilarious thing is that nothing was wrong in our marriage at that particular time, but we were trying to keep it that way—understanding that if we're not growing, we're dying. The strategies outlined in this book will take your marriage from where it is to where you want it to be—all while focusing on leaving a legacy of love for current and future generations. This journey is further simplified when you have a mentor and tribe of like-minded individuals to share it with. Visit crowningdestinies.com for other free resources to assist on your journey.

No marriage is perfect and without challenges. And every marriage is different with different

## My Marriage, My D.E.S.T.I.N.Y.

expectations and different, yet similar challenges. Maybe you're at a place where you've tried everything to get your marriage back on track. You're at the end of your rope, and this was your last attempt before throwing in the towel. If at least one person is willing to make it work, there is still hope. I challenge you to try God. It truly makes everything better. His way is better than anything we could ask or think.

When you implement all of these key strategies: dreaming together, displaying empathy, becoming self-aware, expressing thankfulness and gratitude, embodying integrity, and a newness that fosters yearning for your significant other while also integrating the God factor, you are well on your way to a more harmonious relationship with greater fulfillment, an unshakeable relationship that will last forever. Will you take the easy right or the hard wrong? It's easy to prematurely decide to end your relationship today without evaluating the consequences of tomorrow. This life we live is one with many limitations, but the potential of our impact is limitless. Take control of your

## REFLECTIONS: The God Factor

legacy today, and be that ancestor who adds value for generations to come. When we reach the end of our lives, what we leave behind is far greater than what immediate gratification could ever bring. And always remember that real love stories never end. Touch and agree on this:

My Marriage, My D.E.S.T.I.N.Y.

## PRAYER:

Lord, please strengthen our marriage to be a reflection of You and Your love. Help us to support each other's individual dreams as well as share joint ones. Equip us with the skills necessary to demonstrate empathy and to be more sensitive to one another's needs. Help us to be more self-aware of who You created us to be without devaluing our spouse's individuality. Lord, You know what makes us feel appreciated. Teach us to have a relentless attitude of gratitude while walking in a level of integrity that pleases You. Help us to constantly seek ways to keep our relationship new and alive, so that we have a never-ending yearning for one another and leave a legacy for future generations—our marital destiny. In Jesus' Name we pray, Amen!

## **Acknowledgements**

I would like to tell my grandmother, Erma Jean McClarty, the 92-year-old matriarch of my family, thank you for being my best friend and loving me unconditionally. I love you dearly, and I am so grateful for your support and the special relationship we share.

My mommy dearest, Patricia Bennett has been my rock and sounding board through it all. Thank you for your undying love, support, encouragement and belief in me since I first shared my vision with you. You made all the difference in me becoming the strong, independent and determined woman I am today, and I'll always love and cherish you for the beautiful woman you are—inside and out.

I want to say thank you to my "Poppy," John Bennett for filling in the gap and accepting and loving me as your own. You may not have given me birth, but it is no secret that we are willing to go to the ends of the earth for one another. For that I am grateful beyond measure.

## My Marriage, My D.E.S.T.I.N.Y.

A special thanks to my family for extending your love and support. You've supported me whether I was within driving distance or thousands of miles across the ocean. I could always depend on you all to share in my military separations and my military celebrations. Your contributions were never too small for me to notice, and I found renewed strength from your love and support over the years.

I would be remiss if I didn't express gratitude to my late mother and father-in-love. Both of them loved, received and accepted me from our very first day we were introduced. They are no longer here, but they left an incredible legacy that lives on. I am so grateful they blessed me with such a jewel in their eldest son, Russell Anthony Collins.

Last but not least I must say "thanks be to God who giveth me the victory through our Lord Jesus Christ." (1 Cor 15:57, KJV) Thank you, God, for your inspiration and for breathing life into this vision for it is in You that "I live, move and have (my) being." (Acts 17:28, KJV)

**Tonya Loving Collins**

My Marriage, My D.E.S.T.I.N.Y.

## About the Author

A native of Fort Worth, Texas, Tonya Loving Collins is based out of the greater San Antonio area, where she remained after successfully completing a distinguished 23+ year Army career around the globe. Tonya served in various positions throughout her career including combat deployments in support of Operations Desert Shield and Storm and again in Baghdad, Iraq where she commanded a personnel services element during Operation Iraqi Freedom.

Tonya has always been a go-getter and rose from the rank of Private First Class to Sergeant, retiring as an Army Lieutenant Colonel. She completed both the Adjutant General Officer's Basic Course and Captain's Career Course with academic and physical fitness honors among the many formal military schools she attended. Tonya received numerous awards and decorations throughout her illustrious military

## About the Author

career including the parachutist and air assault badges.

A lifelong learner Tonya matriculated with a Master's Degree in Management Information Systems, a Master's Degree in Human Resources Management, and a Bachelor's Degree in Business Administration. She has a heart for people and serving, and she founded and received the vision for Crowning Destinies, LLC following a difficult transition from the military. Tonya is a Life and Business Strategist, Transformational Speaker, Marriage Enrichment Leader, Mentor, Certified Success Coach, Certified Master Trainer, and Certified DISC Behavioral Trainer. She is committed to fulfilling her calling to empower women and couples to design the best versions of themselves, so they too may live a life of passion and purpose in accordance with their destinies.

Tonya is blessed indeed but will never forget her humble beginnings. She has a servant heart and embodies the philosophy of "learning, living, and then leading" others to a greater life of

## My Marriage, My D.E.S.T.I.N.Y.

fulfillment. While Tonya is grateful for a successful military career, she is elated to walk in her calling—a journey she does not take lightly and finds quite liberating. Of all the titles she's held, her proudest titles are devoted wife of 21 years to Russell and the daily opportunity to guide Rashelle and Rashon toward their purpose as Mom. Last, but certainly not least, Tonya is deeply honored to be connected as a child of the Most High King.

About the Author

# Review Ask

Love this book? Please don't forget to leave a review! Every review matters, and it matters a lot!

Please take a moment and head over to Amazon or wherever you purchased this book to leave an honest review for me. Upon completion, email me your review at [info@crowningdestinies.com](mailto:info@crowningdestinies.com) for entry into a special drawing for a limited time. Thanks in advance for sharing your feedback.

My Marriage, My D.E.S.T.I.N.Y.

Want to work with me or book me to speak or train at your next event?
For information, visit:

WWW.CROWNINGDESTINIES.COM

## About the Author

My Marriage, My D.E.S.T.I.N.Y.

# **Endnotes**

---

[i] ***Covey, Stephen (2013).*** *The 7 Habits of Highly Effective People: Powerful Lessons in Personal Change. New York: Simon & Schuster.*

[ii] *Wevorce (Jan 9, 2017).*
*https://www.wevorce.com/blog/why-are-so-many-people-in-an-unhappy-marriage/*

[iii] *Paterson, Katherine (2001). The Invisible Child. New York: Dutton Children's Publishing.*

[iv] *Chapman, Gary (2015) The 5 Love Languages. Chicago: Northfield Publishing.*


*Scripture quotations are taken from various versions of The Holy Bible; these versions are annotated in each citation that appears within the text.*

Made in the USA
Coppell, TX
30 December 2021